To

From

Date

A New Day

Our purpose at Howard Books is to:

- *Increase faith* in the hearts of growing Christians
- *Inspire holiness* in the lives of believers
- *Instill hope* in the hearts of struggling people everywhere

Because He's coming again!

HOWARD BOOKS

Howard Books, a division of Simon & Schuster, Inc.
1230 Avenue of the Americas, New York, NY 10020
www.howardpublishing.com

A New Day © 2006 by Sandi Patty

Library of Congress Cataloging-in-Publication Data

Patty, Sandi, 1956–
   A new day : a guided journal / Sandi Patty.
   p. cm.
   ISBN 978-1-4516-4331-2

   1. Spiritual journals—Authorship. 2. Spiritual life—Christianity. 3. Bible—Devotional use. 4. Bible—Quotations. I. Title.
BV4509.5.P375 2006
242'.2—dc22

                                                                                        2006049503

10 9 8 7 6 5 4 3 2 1

For information regarding special discounts for bulk purchases, please contact Simon & Schuster Special Sales at 1-800-456-6798 or business@simonandschuster.com

Edited by Sue Ann Jones
Cover design by Matt Smart, The Puckett Group
Interior design by Stephanie D. Walker

Scripture not otherwise marked is from the *Holy Bible, New International Version*®. Copyright © 1973, 1978, 1984 by the International Bible Society. Used by permission of Zondervan. All rights reserved. Other Scripture quotations are from the following sources: *The Amplified ® Bible* (AMP), copyright © 1954, 1958, 1962, 1964, 1965, 1987 by The Lockman Foundation (www.Lockman. org). Used by permission. *The Holy Bible, New Century Version* (NCV), copyright © 1987, 1988, 1991 by Word Publishing, Dallas, Texas 75234. Used by permission. *Holy Bible, New Living Translation* (NLT), copyright 1996. Used by permission of Tyndale House Publishers, Inc., Wheaton, Illinois 60189. All rights reserved. *The King James Version of the Bible* (KJV). *The Living Bible* (TLB), copyright © 1971 by Tyndale House Publishers, Wheaton, Illinois 60189. Used by permission. *The Message* (MSG), © 1993, 1994, 1995, 1996, 2000, 2001, 2002. Used by permission of Navpress Publishing Group. *The New American Standard Bible* (NASB®), copyright © 1960, 1962, 1963, 1968, 1971, 1972, 1973, 1975, 1977, 1995 by The Lockman Foundation (www.Lockman.org). Used by permission. *The New King James Version* (NKJV®), copyright © 1979, 1980, 1982, Thomas Nelson, Inc., Publishers.

For more information about Sandi Patty, go to www.sandipatty.com
For bookings, contact: William Morris Agency, 615-963-3000
Management information: Mike Atkins Entertainment, 615-345-4554

SANDI PATTY

A New Day

A GUIDED JOURNAL

 HOWARD BOOKS
A DIVISION OF SIMON & SCHUSTER
New York   London   Toronto   Sydney

I say, "My splendor is gone
and all that I had hoped from
the LORD."

I remember my affliction and my
wandering,
the bitterness and the gall.
I well remember them,
and my soul is downcast within me.
Yet this I call to mind
and therefore I have hope:
Because of the LORD's great love we
are not consumed,
for his compassions never fail.
They are new every morning;
great is your faithfulness.

—LAMENTATIONS 3:18–23

A Fresh Start with Each New Day

KEEPING A JOURNAL is writing the story of your life as it unfolds. Good and bad, happy and sad, silly and profound.

I'm blessed with an extraordinarily happy life today, but there have been seasons of my life I'd rather forget, seasons when my soul has been "downcast within me." Yet I've learned the value of remembering the hard times as well as the joyful moments, and a journal helps me do that. You see, it's only by looking back that we can appreciate the difficulties we've overcome, the fears we've conquered, the lessons we've learned. It's only by looking back that we can see that single set of footprints in the sand, the footprints of the Savior as he carried us when weakness stole our strength.

When I review the random writings and journal jottings I've made throughout my life, I see again and again the most blessed gift God gives to all of us each morning and throughout the day: the promise of a second chance, a new beginning, a fresh start.

Because of his great love, we are not consumed by the challenges that confront us, the mistakes we make, or the losses we endure. His compassions *never* fail. And every new day that dawns brings us another gift of grace, another opportunity to try again.

I've put together this guided journal hoping you'll find it an inviting, comfortable place to write the story of your life, one day at a time, during the next one hundred days. It's "guided" because the Scripture passage and accompanying thought from me to you have been selected to encourage and inspire you to write. They're intended as a little spark to ignite your spirit and encourage you to record your thoughts and prayers, especially on those days when you may think you have nothing to say. I hope you'll let God's Word—and my gentle prompting—get you started.

When these pages are full, you'll have recorded a chapter of your personal history. I hope it's one you'll enjoy reading and rereading in the years ahead, finding in your own words the insight and wisdom gleaned from one hundred new days, well lived.

Sandi Patty

Date _____

Behold, I am doing a new thing!
—Isaiah 43:19 AMP

A fresh start, a different perspective, a better outlook . . . whatever "new" looks like for you,
God can do it! He is the God of new beginnings and second chances.

Date _____

I thank my God every time I remember you.
—PHILIPPIANS 1:3

When I remember those who have nurtured my goodness, encouraged my talent, shared my burdens, and taught me how to love, I realize . . . I am blessed!

Date _____

May the God of hope fill you with all joy and peace as you trust in him,
so that you may overflow with hope by the power of the Holy Spirit.
—ROMANS 15:13

Even in difficult times, we can trust the God of hope to fill us with joy and peace. Even on the darkest days, we turn toward the Light and are filled by his radiant presence.

Date _____

_____

_____

_____

_____

_____

_____

_____

_____

_____

_____

_____

_____

_____

_____

_____

_____

_____

_____

_____

In him all things hold together.
—Colossians 1:17

When things seem to fall apart, remember that the One who holds the universe together also holds our lives in his hands. In his grip, we find the strength to take one more step.

Date _____

_____

_____

_____

_____

_____

_____

_____

_____

_____

_____

_____

_____

_____

_____

_____

_____

_____

_____

_____

When others are happy, be happy with them. If they are sad, share their sorrow.
—ROMANS 12:15 NLT

We are created in God's image. He rejoices with us in good times and comforts us in our sorrow—and then he urges us to do the same with one another.

Date

The LORD your God is with you, he is mighty to save. He will take great delight in you,
he will quiet you with his love, he will rejoice over you with singing.
—ZEPHANIAH 3:17

Imagine! The Creator of the universe delights in you. He quiets your worries with his powerful love and serenades you in his joy. You must be really special!

Date _____

Be joyful always.
—1 Thessalonians 5:16

When things aren't going the way I want them to, my kids tell me, "Mom, you've gotta find the joy!" And what do you know? That's what God tells me too!

Date _____

Anxious hearts are very heavy but a word of encouragement does wonders!
—Proverbs 12:25 TLB

How thankful I am for a kind word in the midst of misery. How uplifting it is to be encouraged on dark days. Oh God, help me pass on the gift!

Date

God has not given us a spirit of fear and timidity, but of power, love, and self-discipline.
—2 TIMOTHY 1:7 NLT

What amazing gifts God has given us, gifts that enable us to do extraordinary things.
Hmmmmm. What extraordinary thing will I do today?

Date _____

_____

_____

_____

_____

_____

_____

_____

_____

_____

_____

_____

_____

_____

_____

_____

_____

_____

_____

_____

_____

_____

_____

_____

[Jesus said,] *"If you understand what I'm telling you, act like it—and live a blessed life."*
—JOHN 13:17 MSG

Note to self: You're not just anybody. You're God's child, a sinner saved by grace, and an earthly representative of the King of kings. Go out there and act like it!

Date _____

_____

_____

_____

_____

_____

_____

_____

_____

_____

_____

_____

_____

_____

_____

_____

_____

_____

_____

_____

The eternal God is your refuge, and underneath are the everlasting arms.
—DEUTERONOMY 33:27 NKJV

I cherish the peace I find in the security of God's steadfast embrace.

Date_____

_____

_____

_____

_____

_____

_____

_____

_____

_____

_____

_____

_____

_____

_____

_____

_____

_____

_____

_____

_____

Whatever you do, work at it with all your heart, as working for the Lord, not for men.
—Colossians 3:23

Whether I'm driving carpool, waiting in line, or performing in the spotlight,
help me remember, Lord, that I'm doing it for you.

Date _____

_____

_____

_____

_____

_____

_____

_____

_____

_____

_____

_____

_____

_____

_____

_____

_____

_____

_____

_____

_____

_____

_____

You saw what he did in the wilderness, how GOD, your God, carried you as a father carries
his child, carried you the whole way until you arrived here.
—DEUTERONOMY 1:31 MSG

God faithfully carries me through the wilderness of worry
and the desert of dread, and into the glory of his promises.

Date

If anyone is in Christ, he is a new creation; the old has gone, the new has come!
—2 CORINTHIANS 5:17

What's done is done. The important thing is, what will you do now? The old you is gone.
What will the new you do in this new day?

Date _____

Draw near to God and He will draw near to you.
—JAMES 4:8 NKJV

God's presence in my life is a constant source of loving encouragement and soothing peace.

Date _____

Do not forget to entertain strangers, for by so doing some have unwittingly entertained angels.
—Hebrews 13:1–2 NKJV

May I have the eyes to see "stranger angels" throughout this day,
and may I be alert to ways to be an "angel" to someone else.

Date _____

_____
_____
_____
_____
_____
_____
_____
_____
_____
_____
_____
_____
_____
_____
_____
_____
_____
_____
_____
_____

Let your gentleness be evident to all.
—PHILIPPIANS 4:5

Even when life gets hurried and hassled,
may we show patience and gentleness in everything we do.

Date _____

_____

_____

_____

_____

_____

_____

_____

_____

_____

_____

_____

_____

_____

_____

_____

_____

_____

_____

_____

_____

_____

Make haste, O Lord, to help me.
—Psalm 40:13 NASB

How reassuring to know that whether I'm crying secretly on the back row of the balcony or publicly mired in misery, God is always on call to rescue me.

Date _____

_____

_____

_____

_____

_____

_____

_____

_____

_____

_____

_____

_____

_____

_____

_____

_____

_____

_____

_____

_____

Give, and it will be given to you. A good measure, pressed down, shaken together and running over, will be poured into your lap.
—LUKE 6:38

May we be as generous in sharing our blessings as God has been in blessing us.

Date _____

_____

_____

_____

_____

_____

_____

_____

_____

_____

_____

_____

_____

_____

_____

_____

_____

_____

_____

_____

_____

_____

_____

_____

When you pass through the waters, I will be with you; and when you pass through
the rivers, they will not sweep over you.
—ISAIAH 43:2

We can sail forth into each day with confidence and courage, knowing God is at the helm.

Date _____

_____

_____

_____

_____

_____

_____

_____

_____

_____

_____

_____

_____

_____

_____

_____

_____

_____

_____

_____

Whether you turn to the right or to the left, your ears will hear a voice behind you, saying,
"This is the way; walk in it."
—ISAIAH 30:21

Amid the hubbub of my busy life, may I always hear God's voice in my ear.

Date _____

_____

_____

_____

_____

_____

_____

_____

_____

_____

_____

_____

_____

_____

_____

_____

_____

_____

_____

_____

_____

_____

_____

She said to herself, "If I only touch his cloak, I will be healed."
—MATTHEW 9:21

Oh, to have the faith of that woman!

Date _____

_____

_____

_____

_____

_____

_____

_____

_____

_____

_____

_____

_____

_____

_____

_____

_____

_____

_____

_____

_____

_____

_____

Do not let your hearts be troubled and do not be afraid.
—JOHN 14:27

Tonight I will hand Jesus my heartache and my fear,
and I will lay down my head to sleep in peace.

Date _____

_May our Lord Jesus Christ himself and God our Father, who loved us
and by his grace gave us eternal encouragement and good hope,
encourage your hearts and strengthen you in every good deed and word._
—2 Thessalonians 2:16–17

Let me pass on God's extraordinary encouragement to others . . .

Date _____

_____
_____
_____
_____
_____
_____
_____
_____
_____
_____
_____
_____
_____
_____
_____
_____
_____
_____
_____
_____
_____
_____

Therefore, since we have such a hope, we are very bold.
—2 CORINTHIANS 3:12

My hope is in you, Lord. Show me how I can be "very bold" on your behalf.

Date _____

He was in the desert forty days, being tempted by Satan.
He was with the wild animals, and angels attended him.
—MARK 1:13

I count my blessings and recognize the gifts I've been given,
and I'm blown away by God's gracious goodness to me.

Date

Don't be afraid; just believe.
—Luke 8:50

Wherever I go today—and every day—I want to feel God's reassuring presence around me.

Date _____

_____

_____

_____

_____

_____

_____

_____

_____

_____

_____

_____

_____

_____

_____

_____

_____

_____

_____

_____

This is too much, too wonderful—I can't take it all in!
—PSALM 139:6 MSG

Worry is a waste of time and energy. Help me remember that, Lord,
and keep my thoughts focused on you.

Date _____

_____

_____

_____

_____

_____

_____

_____

_____

_____

_____

_____

_____

_____

_____

_____

_____

_____

_____

_____

_____

I'm an open book to you; even from a distance, you know what I'm thinking.
—PSALM 139:2 MSG

God knows our innermost secrets, the motivation behind our actions, the fears and yearnings of our hearts. He knows what I will write here before I pick up the pen.

Date _____

_____

_____

_____

_____

_____

_____

_____

_____

_____

_____

_____

_____

_____

_____

_____

_____

_____

_____

_____

_____

You know when I leave and when I get back; I'm never out of your sight.
—PSALM 139:3 MSG

This thing I have to do seems too big, too difficult,
too much. I can't do it . . . unless God helps me.

Date _____

_____

_____

_____

_____

_____

_____

_____

_____

_____

_____

_____

_____

_____

_____

_____

_____

_____

May God himself . . . make you holy and whole, put you together—
spirit, soul, and body—and keep you fit.
—1 Thessalonians 5:23 MSG

When life seems to be falling apart, turn to the One who created all of life and feel yourself being restored to wholeness.

Date _____

As welcoming as a porch light glowing late at night,
God's attentive love wraps us in peace wherever we travel.

Date

You know everything I'm going to say before I start the first sentence.
—Psalm 139:4 MSG

How God must cringe sometimes, knowing what's about to come out of my mouth!
Help me remember, Lord: pray first, then speak!

Date _____

_____

_____

_____

_____

_____

_____

_____

_____

_____

_____

_____

_____

_____

_____

_____

_____

_____

_____

_____

_____

I look behind me and you're there, then up ahead and you're there, too—
your reassuring presence, coming and going.
—PSALM 139:5 MSG

What a blessing it is to have someone who understands our pain
and weakness come alongside us and lead us toward the Light.

Date _____

_____

_____

_____

_____

_____

_____

_____

_____

_____

_____

_____

_____

_____

_____

_____

_____

_____

_____

_____

Don't get worked up about what may or may not happen tomorrow.
God will help you deal with whatever hard things come up when the time comes.
—MATTHEW 6:34–35 MSG

Whatever today holds for me, I will remember I'm glory-bound!

Date _____

_____

_____

_____

_____

_____

_____

_____

_____

_____

_____

_____

_____

_____

_____

_____

_____

_____

_____

_____

_____

_____

_____

_____

_____

What are mere mortals, that you should make so much of us?
—JOB 7:17 NLT

On a starlit night, my daughter Jennifer and I watched a falling star
and shrieked with delight, feeling like honored spectators—
a private, privileged audience admiring God's glorious show.

Date _____

_____

_____

_____

_____

_____

_____

_____

_____

_____

_____

_____

_____

_____

_____

_____

_____

_____

_____

_____

_____

Now glory be to God! By his mighty power at work within us, he is able to accomplish infinitely more than we would ever dare to ask or hope.
—EPHESIANS 3:20 NLT

There's something I want to do. On my own, it would be impossible, but if it's God's will to help me, I know I can accomplish anything I dare to hope for.

Date

O God, You are my God; early will I seek You.
—Psalm 63:1 NKJV

I open my eyes each morning and think of my dear Father.
May I be aware of him in everyone I see and everything I do today.

Date _____

_____

_____

_____

_____

_____

_____

_____

_____

_____

_____

_____

_____

_____

_____

_____

_____

_____

_____

_____

_____

_____

Jesus Christ is the same yesterday and today and forever.
—HEBREWS 13:8

Life changes so quickly. Children grow. Moods swing. Fashions flip. Terror strikes. Yet amid the changes, there is One who is faithful and true, dependable and trustworthy.

Date _____

Lo, I am with you alway, even unto the end of the world.
—MATTHEW 28:20 KJV

To know he's there, always and forever, gives us courage
and strength to face whatever comes next.

Date

Make a joyful noise unto the LORD.
—PSALM 100:1 KJV

No matter what kind of "joyful noise" of praise we offer him, to God's ear it's beautiful.

Date _____

_____

_____

_____

_____

_____

_____

_____

_____

_____

_____

_____

_____

_____

_____

_____

_____

_____

_____

_____

_____

_____

_____

Pray without ceasing.
—1 Thessalonians 5:17 KJV

*Dear Lord, let every word I speak and everything I do today
be a prayer of praise and thankfulness to you.*

Date _____

May the Golden Rule govern everyone's heart, including mine.

Date _____

_____

_____

_____

_____

_____

_____

_____

_____

_____

_____

_____

_____

_____

_____

_____

_____

_____

I tell you the truth, he who believes has everlasting life.
—JOHN 6:47

When life here seems bleak, I remember the bright future God has promised me in heaven.

Date _____

_____

_____

_____

_____

_____

_____

_____

_____

_____

_____

_____

_____

_____

_____

_____

_____

_____

_____

_____

_____

Lord, I do not deserve to have you come under my roof.
But just say the word, and my servant will be healed.
—MATTHEW 8:7–8

Oh, to have the sincere humility and unshakable faith of that centurion!

Date _____

Old friends avoid me like the plague.
—Psalm 38:11 MSG

Lord, as one who knows too well the agony of being condemned and shunned,
help me share today your wonderful gift of hope and grace with someone who's hurting.

Date_____

_____

_____

_____

_____

_____

_____

_____

_____

_____

_____

_____

_____

_____

_____

_____

_____

_____

_____

The fire of love stops at nothing—it sweeps everything before it.
—Song of Solomon 8:6 MSG

My heart overflows with the gracious and magnificent love of God.

Date _____

The ones who do the planting or watering aren't important,
but God is important because he is the one who makes the seed grow.
—1 CORINTHIANS 3:7 NLT

When applause reaches my ears, I will remember that whatever talent I may possess is God's gift and not my solitary accomplishment.

Date

We are hunted down, but God never abandons us.
We get knocked down, but we get up again and keep going.
—2 CORINTHIANS 4:9 NLT

In my darkest hours, I feel courage, comfort, and assurance in the Lord's powerful presence.

Date _____

_____

_____

_____

_____

_____

_____

_____

_____

_____

_____

_____

_____

_____

_____

_____

_____

_____

_____

_____

_____

_____

May God be gracious to us and bless us and make his face shine upon us.
—PSALM 67:1

What joy it brings to think of my Creator's face shining upon me!

Date _____

_____

_____

_____

_____

_____

_____

_____

_____

_____

_____

_____

_____

_____

_____

_____

_____

_____

_____

_____

_____

_____

_____

The LORD is my strength and my song.
—PSALM 118:14

In anxious times, I hear God's sweet song of love in my heart
and feel comforted by his mighty and delightful presence.

Date _____

_____
_____
_____
_____
_____
_____
_____
_____
_____
_____
_____
_____
_____
_____
_____
_____
_____
_____
_____
_____
_____

The LORD is compassionate and gracious, slow to anger, abounding in love.
—PSALM 103:8

You set high standards, Lord! As a busy mother and wife,
I need your constant help to follow in your footsteps.

Date _____

_____

_____

_____

_____

_____

_____

_____

_____

_____

_____

_____

_____

_____

_____

_____

_____

_____

You should be known for the beauty that comes from within, the unfading beauty
of a gentle and quiet spirit, which is so precious to God.
—1 Peter 3:4 NLT

_I hope every note I sing, every word I speak, and everything I do helps others
find God's precious gift of a gentle and quiet spirit._

Date

It is by grace you have been saved, through faith—
and this not from yourselves, it is the gift of God.
—EPHESIANS 2:8

Try as I might, I can't save myself.
The only lifeline strong enough to save me is God's extraordinary gift of grace.

Date _____

Worship the LORD in all his holy splendor.
—1 CHRONICLES 16:29 NLT

I worship you, Lord, with all my heart, body, soul, and song!
I praise your holy name forever. Amen.

Date _____

_____

_____

_____

_____

_____

_____

_____

_____

_____

_____

_____

_____

_____

_____

_____

_____

_____

_____

_____

_____

_____

Cast all your anxiety on him because he cares for you.
—1 Peter 5:7

Today I drop my burdens at God's feet, then picture myself being enfolded in his everlasting arms to find eternal rest and peace.

Date _____

_____

_____

_____

_____

_____

_____

_____

_____

_____

_____

_____

_____

_____

_____

_____

_____

_____

_____

I know what it is to be in need, and I know what it is to have plenty.
I have learned the secret of being content in any and every situation.
—PHILIPPIANS 4:12

My life in God is the secret of my contentment, no matter my circumstances.
That's one secret I won't keep to myself!

Date _____

_____

_____

_____

_____

_____

_____

_____

_____

_____

_____

_____

_____

_____

_____

_____

_____

_____

_____

_____

As God's chosen people, holy and dearly loved,
clothe yourselves with compassion, kindness, humility, gentleness and patience.
—COLOSSIANS 3:12

Today I will strive to share with others the gifts God has given me as his dearly loved child: compassion, kindness, humility, gentleness, and patience.

Date

Unless the LORD builds the house, its builders labor in vain.
—PSALM 127:1

Families come home for rest, nourishment, and companionship.
But the best thing found in the heart of a godly home is God's comforting peace.

Date _____

_____
_____
_____
_____
_____
_____
_____
_____
_____
_____
_____
_____
_____
_____
_____
_____
_____
_____
_____

"I know the plans I have for you," declares the LORD, "plans to prosper you and not to harm you, plans to give you hope and a future."
—JEREMIAH 29:11

_When things go wrong, when my plans fail, I cling to God's promises and wait for him
to reveal his plan for my prosperous, hopeful future._

Date _____

His love endures forever.
—1 CHRONICLES 16:34

The strongest force the universe has ever known: God's amazing love. How blessed I am to be enfolded in its immeasurable, indescribable goodness.

Date _____

You heard my cry for mercy when I called to you for help.
—PSALM 31:22

*How reassuring it is to know God is listening for my voice
and stands ready to respond to my cry for help.*

Date _____

_____

_____

_____

_____

_____

_____

_____

_____

_____

_____

_____

_____

_____

_____

_____

_____

_____

_____

My soul is weary with sorrow; strengthen me according to your word.
—Psalm 119:28

When heartache arrives unexpectedly, I am grief-stricken and fearful.
Give me strength, dear Jesus, to keep breathing . . . and keep believing.

You are God my Savior, and my hope is in you all day long.
—PSALM 25:5

All day long, whenever fear arises or anxiety besets me,
I will remember that God brings me peace, even in times of crisis.

Date _____

_____

_____

_____

_____

_____

_____

_____

_____

_____

_____

_____

_____

_____

_____

_____

_____

_____

_____

_____

_____

_____

_____

Our mouths were filled with laughter, our tongues with songs of joy.
—Psalm 126:2

What joy I feel, remembering happy times with my loved ones.
Thank you, Lord, for this wonderful, crazy family of mine!

Date _____

_____

_____

_____

_____

_____

_____

_____

_____

_____

_____

_____

_____

_____

_____

_____

_____

_____

_____

_____

_____

Every detail in our lives of love for God is worked into something good.
—ROMANS 8:28 MSG

Oh Lord, the mistakes I make! But when your loving spirit fills my heart,
you turn my mixed-up moves into a beautiful ballet of goodness.

Date _____

What is impossible with men is possible with God.
—LUKE 18:27

Help me remember, Lord, today's challenges are gifts, and you're with me as I open them.

Date _____

_____

_____

_____

_____

_____

_____

_____

_____

_____

_____

_____

_____

_____

_____

_____

_____

_____

_____

_____

_____

_____

_____

This is a spiritual refining process, with glory just around the corner.
—1 PETER 4:13 MSG

_I think of the "angels" God has sent to tend me in the "deserts" of my life—friends,
family members, and strangers—and I'm grateful for each one._

Date _____

_____

_____

_____

_____

_____

_____

_____

_____

_____

_____

_____

_____

_____

_____

_____

_____

_____

_____

_____

_____

_____

Consider it a sheer gift, friends, when tests and challenges come at you from all sides. You know that under pressure, your faith-life is forced into the open and shows its true colors.
—JAMES 1:2–3 MSG

Whisper these words in my heart all day and all night, dear God,
as I face problems and challenges.

Date _____

_____

_____

_____

_____

_____

_____

_____

_____

_____

_____

_____

_____

_____

_____

_____

_____

_____

_____

_____

_____

_____

The LORD is in his holy temple; let all the earth be silent before him.
—HABAKKUK 2:20

We worship God with our voices, our music, our actions—and also with our reverent silence.

Date _____

_____

_____

_____

_____

_____

_____

_____

_____

_____

_____

_____

_____

_____

_____

_____

_____

_____

Sorrow and mourning will disappear, and they will be overcome with joy and gladness.
—ISAIAH 35:10 NLT

Our loving God wipes away our tears and fills our broken hearts with laughter.

*So overflowing is his kindness towards us that he took away all our sins
through the blood of his Son.*
—EPHESIANS 1:7 TLB

_What freedom we have, humbly realizing our sins
have been erased by Jesus's extraordinary sacrifice!_

Date _____

He has showered down upon us the richness of his grace—
for how well he understands us and knows what is best for us at all times.
—EPHESIANS 1:8 TLB

God knows me through and through . . . and loves me anyway!

Date _____

In the midst of crisis, wait and watch to discern God's omniscient guidance.

Date _____

_____

_____

_____

_____

_____

_____

_____

_____

_____

_____

_____

_____

_____

_____

_____

_____

_____

_____

_____

_____

Anyone by just giving you a cup of water in my name is on our side.
Count on it that God will notice.
—MARK 9:41 MSG

Even the smallest good deed done in Jesus's name can have a big impact . . .
because God is watching.

Date _____

How wonderful to be a child of the God of second chances and new beginnings!

Date _____

_____

_____

_____

_____

_____

_____

_____

_____

_____

_____

_____

_____

_____

_____

_____

_____

_____

_____

_____

_____

Though I have fallen, I will rise. Though I sit in darkness, the Lord will be my light.
—MICAH 7:8

Thank God! For believers, failure is only a temporary condition,
a darkness that vanishes when the Lord's light shines on us.

Date _____

When a [woman] is gloomy, everything seems to go wrong;
when [she] is cheerful, everything seems right!
—PROVERBS 15:15 TLB

Help me remember, Lord, that my mood affects my family's attitude—
and with as many children as we have, that's a lot of attitude!

Date _____

May your unfailing love rest upon us, O Lord, even as we put our hope in you.
—PSALM 33:22

What precious gifts God has given us: unfailing love and boundless hope!

Date _____

_____
_____
_____
_____
_____
_____
_____
_____
_____
_____
_____
_____
_____
_____
_____
_____
_____
_____
_____
_____
_____
_____
_____
_____
_____
_____

*No eye has seen, no ear has heard, no mind has conceived
what God has prepared for those who love him.*
—1 CORINTHIANS 2:9

During difficult days, I try to think how glorious heaven will be,
even as I realize it will be better than anything my earthly mind can imagine.

Date

*The Father of compassion and the God of all comfort . . . comforts us in all our troubles,
so that we can comfort those in any trouble with the comfort
we ourselves have received from God.*

—2 CORINTHIANS 1:3–4

We're blessed so that we can pass on the blessing,
encouraging the brokenhearted with the same godly encouragement we've received.

Date _____

I know that you sincerely trust the Lord,
for you have the faith of your mother . . . and your grandmother.
—2 TIMOTHY 1:5 NLT

_____

_____

_____

_____

_____

_____

_____

_____

_____

_____

_____

_____

_____

_____

_____

_____

_____

_____

_____

_____

_____

_____

_____

*The strong faith that my mother and grandmother handed down to me
is the legacy I now pass on to my children.*

Date _____

_____

_____

_____

_____

_____

_____

_____

_____

_____

_____

_____

_____

_____

_____

_____

_____

_____

_____

_____

_____

_____

_____

_____

_____

As for me and my house, we will serve the Lord.
—JOSHUA 24:15 KJV

There is no happier time or place for me than when I'm in church, surrounded by my family (we take up a whole pew, all by ourselves!), worshiping God together.

Date _____

_____

_____

_____

_____

_____

_____

_____

_____

_____

_____

_____

_____

_____

_____

_____

_____

_____

_____

_____

_____

Encourage one another and build each other up.
—1 Thessalonians 5:11

Lord, please lead me to someone who needs an uplifting message of encouragement today;
then give me the right words to say.

Date _____

_____

_____

_____

_____

_____

_____

_____

_____

_____

_____

_____

_____

_____

_____

_____

_____

_____

Be merciful, just as your Father is merciful.
—LUKE 6:36

To experience God's mercy is a marvelous thing.
To extend it to others . . . well, that's not always easy. Help me, Lord!

Date _____

_____

_____

_____

_____

_____

_____

_____

_____

_____

_____

_____

_____

_____

_____

_____

_____

_____

_____

_____

_____

_____

_____

_____

In everything you do, put God first, and he will direct you and crown your efforts with success.
—PROVERBS 3:6 TLB

*Great possibilities and unlimited opportunities are open to us
when we put God first in our lives.*

Date _____

I have written your name on my hand.
—Isaiah 49:16 NLT

Imagine! My name is written on the hand of the One who created the universe. Yours is too!

Date _____

_____

_____

_____

_____

_____

_____

_____

_____

_____

_____

_____

_____

_____

_____

_____

_____

_____

_____

_____

_____

_____

_____

_____

God has blessed me with laughter.
—GENESIS 21:6 MSG

If Sarah, the Old Testament heroine, could laugh about being pregnant in her old age,
surely the rest of us can laugh about nearly anything!

Date _____

_____

_____

_____

_____

_____

_____

_____

_____

_____

_____

_____

_____

_____

_____

_____

_____

_____

_____

_____

_____

_____

Put out of your life every evil thing and every kind of wrong.
Then in gentleness accept God's teaching that is planted in your hearts, which can save you.
—JAMES 1:21 NCV

In my heart, I know the right thing to do. Dear God, give me a gentle and gracious spirit to heed your teachings and do that right thing.

Date _____

_____

_____

_____

_____

_____

_____

_____

_____

_____

_____

_____

_____

_____

_____

_____

_____

_____

_____

_____

_____

_____

_____

_____

You'll welcome us with open arms when we run for cover to you.
—PSALM 5:11 MSG

What comfort we find in the safety of God's open arms.

Date _____

_____
_____
_____
_____
_____
_____
_____
_____
_____
_____
_____
_____
_____
_____
_____
_____
_____
_____

Faith is being sure of what we hope for and certain of what we do not see.
—HEBREWS 11:1

Faith is like a tiny candle that gives us just enough light for the next step . . .
because that's all we need when that Light is Jesus.

Date _____

_____

_____

_____

_____

_____

_____

_____

_____

_____

_____

_____

_____

_____

_____

_____

_____

_____

The mountains shall bring peace to the people.
—Psalm 72:3 KJV

What peaceful place do you seek out during stressful times?

Date _____

_____

_____

_____

_____

_____

_____

_____

_____

_____

_____

_____

_____

_____

_____

_____

_____

_____

_____

_____

_____

_____

_____

_____

My soul will rejoice in the Lord and delight in his salvation.
—PSALM 35:9

What happiness I feel, knowing I am God's child: loved, forgiven, and saved.

Last night God's angel stood at my side, . . . saying to me, "Don't give up."
—ACTS 27:23–24 MSG

In the dark night of discouragement, God sends his angels to help me hang on.

Date _____

_____

_____

_____

_____

_____

_____

_____

_____

_____

_____

_____

_____

_____

_____

_____

_____

_____

_____

_____

_____

_____

_____

*Forgetting the past and straining toward what is ahead, I keep trying to reach the goal
and get the prize for which God called me through Christ to the life above.*
—PHILIPPIANS 3:13–14 NCV

Amid life's struggles, we keep our eyes on the goal: spending eternity in heaven with Jesus.

Date _____

_____
_____
_____
_____
_____
_____
_____
_____
_____
_____
_____
_____
_____
_____
_____
_____
_____

So we know and rely on the love God has for us. God is love.
Whoever lives in love lives in God, and God in him.

—1 JOHN 4:16

Our Creator isn't the God of love. He is love.
And he asks us to represent him in everything we do and share him with everyone we know.

Date _____

_____
_____
_____
_____
_____
_____
_____
_____
_____
_____
_____
_____
_____
_____
_____
_____
_____
_____
_____
_____
_____
_____

God is light; in him there is no darkness at all.
—1 JOHN 1:5

The light of God's loving presence soothes us,
encourages us, and sustains us as it pushes back the darkness.

Date _____

_____

_____

_____

_____

_____

_____

_____

_____

_____

_____

_____

_____

_____

_____

_____

_____

_____

_____

_____

_____

*You have been born again. . . . This new life will last forever
because it comes from the eternal, living word of God.*
—1 PETER 1:23 NLT

God's grace means we don't have to worry that we'll make an irreparable mistake.
We acknowledge our failures, seek forgiveness, and begin again.

Date _____

_____

_____

_____

_____

_____

_____

_____

_____

_____

_____

_____

_____

_____

_____

_____

_____

_____

_____

_____

_____

_____

An empty stable stays clean, but no income comes from an empty stable.
—Proverbs 14:4 NLT

In our family of eight children, we've adapted this proverb to say,
An empty house stays clean, but what fun is a clean house?

Date _____

For God so loved the world, that he gave his only begotten Son,
that whosoever believeth in him should not perish, but have everlasting life.
—JOHN 3:16 KJV

Lord, help me live this day—and every day—in honor of your sacrifice.

To learn about Sandi Patty's story of
Hope and New Beginnings,
you'll want to read...

Sandi Patty's tumultuous journey from devastating sin through healing forgive
and into God's incredible grace began on the back row of a church balcony.
book is the heart-touching narrative of her happy childhood, her stellar career
fall from public acclaim, and the steps she worked through with her church to
peace and forgiveness.

> *You don't forget Sandi's voice. But her voice is nothing compared to her heart. It's had its tough times. Guilt, hurt, anger, fear—her heart has felt it all. Yet, through it all, she has continued to sing. If your heart is finding it hard to do the same, my friend Sandi can help.*
>
> —MAX LUCADO, FROM THE FOREWORD